KINGFISHER READERS

Firefighters

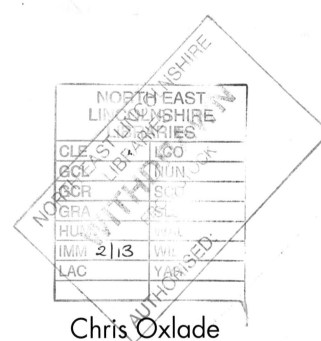

Chris Oxlade

KINGFISHER

First published 2013 by Kingfisher
an imprint of Macmillan Children's Books
a division of Macmillan Publishers Limited
20 New Wharf Road, London N1 9RR
Basingstoke and Oxford
Associated companies throughout the world
www.panmacmillan.com

Series editor: Heather Morris
Literacy consultant: Hilary Horton

ISBN: 978-0-7534-3094-1
Copyright © Macmillan Publishers Ltd 2013

9 8 7 6 5 4 3 2 1

1TR/1012/WKT/UG/105MA

A CIP catalogue record for this book is available from the British Library.

Printed in China

Picture credits
The Publisher would like to thank the following for permission to reproduce their material.
Every care has been taken to trace copyright holders. However, if there have been
unintentional omissions or failure to trace copyright holders, we apologize and will,
if informed, endeavour to make corrections in any future edition.
Top = t; Bottom = b; Centre = c; Left = l; Right = r
Cover Shutterstock/Mike Brake and pages 3t Shutterstock/Monkey Business Images; 3tc
Shutterstock/Zulhazmi Zabri; 3c Shutterstock/Pavel Bortel; 3cb Shutterstock/Will Thomson;
3b Shutterstock/Keith Muratori; 4-5 Shutterstock/Ronald Caswell; 6 Shutterstock/Monkey
Business Images; 7t Getty/Riser; 7b Corbis/Creasource; 8 Shutterstock/mikeledray;
9 Shutterstock/Zulhazmi Zabri; 10 Shutterstock/Monkey Business Images; 11 Shutterstock/
Bryan Eastham; 12 Shutterstock/Jerry Sharp; 14 Shutterstock; 15 Alamy/Alex Ramsay;
16 Shutterstock/Steve Noakes; 17t Shutterstock/TFoxFoto; 17b Shutterstock/Pavel Bortel;
18–19 Shutterstock/Jeff Krushinski; 18 Shutterstock/Keith Muratori; 19 Alamy/Jack Sullivan;
20 Alamy/Ian Marlow; 21t Corbis/Uwe Anspach; 21b Alamy/Sagaphoto; 22 Alamy/Michael
Routh; 23 Shutterstock/Will Thomson; 24 Alamy/Imagebroker; 25 Shutterstock/Gary Blakeley;
28 Shutterstock/Luis Louro; 29 Alamy/Shout; 31 Getty/Riser

Contents

What is a firefighter?

A firefighter is someone who helps in an **emergency**. A firefighter's main job is to put out fires. When a fire starts, a team of firefighters rushes to the fire. The firefighters use hoses, ladders and other **equipment** to put out the fire. They rescue people trapped by fire, too.

Firefighters help with other emergencies. They rescue people after accidents such as car crashes, and also help people trapped in floods or on cliffs by the sea.

Ready and waiting

Firefighters wait at the fire station until they are needed for an emergency. While they wait they clean and mend their fire engines and other equipment, and practise their firefighting skills.

When an emergency call comes in, the firefighters leap into action. They jump into their fire engines as fast as they can. The engines zoom out of the fire station

and head towards the emergency. The driver switches on flashing lights and loud **sirens** to warn people to get out of the way.

Firefighter fact
Some fire stations have a metal pole that firefighters slide down to get to their fire engines quickly.

Training to fight fires

Firefighters train for months before they are allowed to tackle fires. They learn how to work hoses, **pumps**, ladders and all sorts of other equipment. They learn how fires start and how to put fires out. They also learn first aid and how to find people who have been trapped by fires.

Firefighters have to be brave and fit. They learn how to work in places where it's very hot and smoky. They also learn to be part of a firefighting team.

Firefighters train with real fires. Sometimes firefighters set fire to old buildings on purpose. Then they fight the fire to practise using their equipment.

A firefighter learns to run through flames.

Special clothes

Firefighters wear tough jackets and trousers as well as thick gloves when they tackle fires. They are made from special materials that don't catch fire even if flames touch them. They are also waterproof.

Firefighters always wear helmets to protect their heads, and waterproof boots.

Firefighters wear breathing **apparatus** when they go into a building full of smoke. A mask goes over the firefighter's face and connects to a tank of air for the firefighter to breathe.

Firefighter fact
Firefighters put on their trousers, jackets, helmets and boots as they speed along in the fire engine.

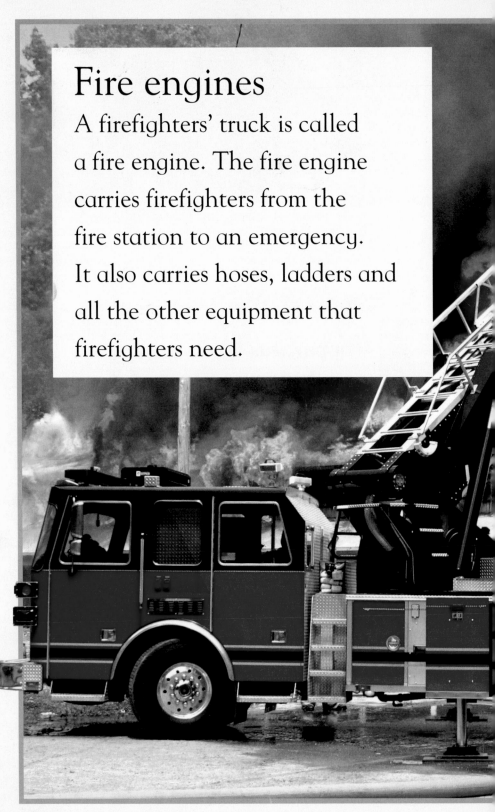

Fire engines

A firefighters' truck is called a fire engine. The fire engine carries firefighters from the fire station to an emergency. It also carries hoses, ladders and all the other equipment that firefighters need.

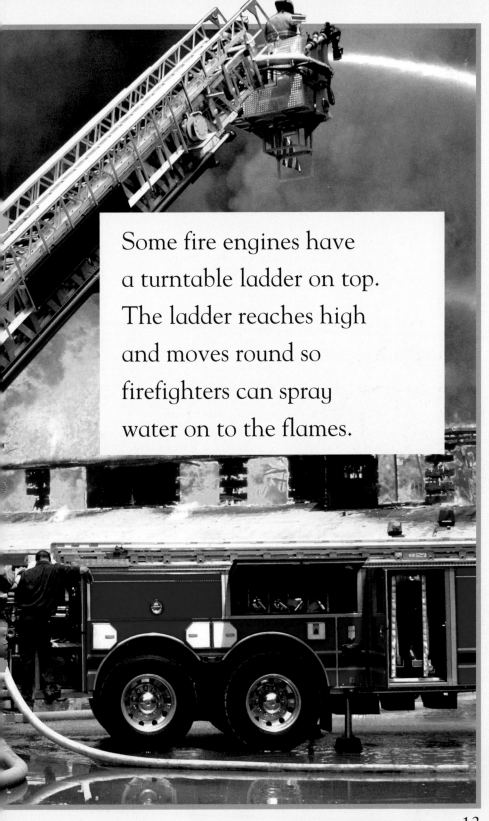

Some fire engines have
a turntable ladder on top.
The ladder reaches high
and moves round so
firefighters can spray
water on to the flames.

Making a plan

When firefighters arrive at an emergency, they jump out, ready for action. The leading firefighter quickly makes a plan, and tells the other firefighters what to do. Some firefighters unroll hoses and connect them to the fire engine's pump. Others unload ladders from the fire engine.

Where do firefighters get water? Sometimes they have a water tank inside their fire engine. In towns they get water from pipes under the street. In the countryside they sometimes take it from rivers or ponds.

Taking water from a **hydrant**

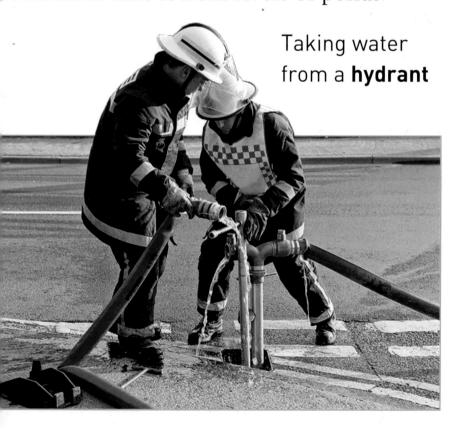

Putting out flames

Firefighters pour water on to fires with hoses. The water cools down the fire, and puts out the flames.

Firefighters don't spray water on burning oil or petrol. The oil or petrol would float on the water and keep burning. So firefighters spray **foam** instead. The foam covers the fire and puts out the flames.

Water comes out of a **nozzle** at the end of a hose. Firefighters have to hold the nozzle tightly because it pushes them backwards as the water rushes out.

A firefighter sprays foam on burning tyres.

Into the smoke

Firefighters have to go into buildings that are on fire. They might have to fight a fire inside a building, or rescue people who are trapped by flames.

The rooms may be full of smoke. The smoke makes people cough and choke.

A firefighter wearing breathing apparatus

Sometimes smoke is poisonous, too. Firefighters always wear breathing apparatus so they can breathe. A mask keeps the stinging smoke out of their eyes.

It is hard to see in smoke. The smoke makes it hard for firefighters to find people who may be trapped. They look through a special camera to help them find people in the smoke.

A fireman uses a camera to search for people in smoke.

Rescue!

Firefighters also help people who are trapped in crashed cars, or in flooded buildings, or on cliffs by the sea.

When someone is trapped in a crashed car, firefighters use tools called **cutters** and **spreaders** to get them out. A cutter is like a giant pair of scissors. It slices easily through the tough metal of a car. A spreader pushes the metal parts of a car apart.

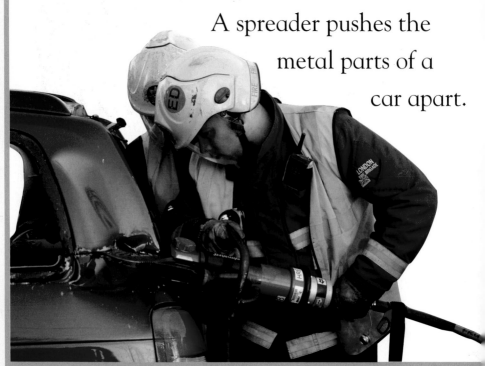

Firefighters use boats to carry people from flooded homes.

They use ropes to rescue people from rivers or stuck on cliffs.

Fighting wildfires

Fires in forest and bush land are called **wildfires**. These fires spread quickly and are tricky to put out. Firefighters have special equipment to tackle wildfires. They travel in off-road fire engines that can drive over rough ground to reach a fire.

A helicopter carries water to a wildfire.

Firefighters also use helicopters and planes to drop water on fires. They often cut down trees to make a gap in the forest and stop a fire spreading.

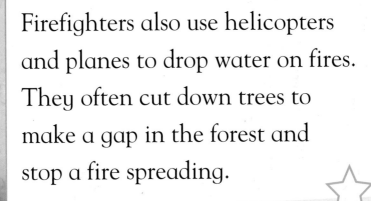

Fighting a forest fire in California, USA

Fire fact
On a windy day, a wildfire can burn through a forest faster than a person can run.

Special firefighting jobs

All airports have a team of firefighters and special fire engines. The team is always ready for action when aircraft are taking off and landing, in case there is an emergency.

Firefighter fact
Firefighting teams in airports practise their skills by setting fire to old aircraft.

An airport fire engine has a cannon on top that sprays foam which will put out burning fuel.

Some firefighters work on boats and ships. These are like fire engines at sea. They put out fires in buildings on the shore, and on ships and oil rigs.

A firefighting boat rushes to a fire.

Firefighters in the past

Hundreds of years ago firefighters used small fire carts. They pulled the carts through the streets to reach a fire, then pumped water along their hoses by hand.

In some cities, people called fire wardens watched for fires from tall towers.

Most buildings were made of wood, which burns easily. The buildings were very close

Firefighter fact
The first firefighters worked in the city of Rome in Italy about 2,000 years ago.

together, so flames could jump from one building to the next. If a fire grew too big, the firefighters couldn't put it out. Sometimes fires destroyed hundreds of houses.

There was a huge fire in London in 1666. Firefighters pulled down houses to try to stop the flames.

Fire safety

Most fires start by accident, when cooking oil catches fire or because electric wires break. Some start when people drop burning cigarettes. Firefighters tell people how to prevent these accidents. They also help people to put up **smoke detectors** and teach them how to use **fire extinguishers**. Firefighters visit homes, schools, offices and factories to talk about fire safety.

Glossary

apparatus Another word for equipment.

cutter A machine that cuts through metal like a pair of powerful scissors.

emergency There is an emergency when someone is in danger and needs help from the fire or ambulance service, or the police.

equipment Things people use to do a job, such as firefighters' hoses and pumps.

fire extinguisher A container of water or foam which is used to put out a small fire.

foam A mass of tiny bubbles.

hydrant A pipe in the street where firefighters can get water for their hoses.

nozzle The pointed end of a pipe.

pump A machine that pushes water along a pipe.

siren A piece of equipment that makes a very loud wailing noise.

smoke detector A machine that makes a loud alarm noise when it senses smoke from a fire.

spreader A machine that pushes apart pieces of metal. Firefighters use spreaders to help people escape from crashed cars.

sprinkler A piece of equipment fixed to the ceiling of a room, which looks like a shower head. A sprinker sprays water if a fire starts in the room.

wildfire A fire in a forest or countryside.

Index